THE
LEFT-HANDED
BOOK

by James T. de Kay

M. Evans & Company, Inc.

New York, New York 10017

"Left-handers have much
   more enthusiasm for life.
   They sleep on the wrong
   side of the bed, and
   their heads become
   stagnant on that side."

   — Casey Stengel

Dedicated to Alexander the Great,
Benjamin Franklin, Babe Ruth,
Hans Holbein, Betty Grable,
Huntington Hartford, Rock
Hudson, Peter Lawford,
Rudy Vallee, Joanne Woodward,
Casey Stengel, Dick Van Dyke,
Harry S. Truman, Ty Cobb,
Judy Garland, Charlemagne,
Milton Caniff, Pablo Picasso,
King George VI, Lord Nelson,
Bill Mauldin, Carmen Basilio,

and half the Beatles (Paul
and Ringo) who are all left-
handed, and to Helen and
Gareth, who are not.

At least one person in ten
is left-handed.

Dr. Bryng Bryngelson, of the
University of Minnesota, says:
"Left-handed people tend to be
more creative, more imaginative
than right-handed people." Which
may explain why Michaelangelo,
Raphael and Leonardo were
all left-handed.

FAMOUS ARTISTS
SCHOOL OF FLORENCE

It doesn't necessarily explain
why Gerald Ford is left-handed.

The human brain is divided
into two hemispheres, and
one dominates the other. If
the right hemisphere dominates,
you'll be left-handed.

Being left-handed in
a right-handed world
can be frustrating,
which may account for
the fact that both
Jack the Ripper and
the Boston Strangler
were left-handed.

This frustration may also
account for the disquieting
statistic that left-handers
are 3 times more apt to
become alcoholics.

Just look
at the
problems
they face…

Left-handed violinists, 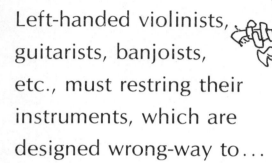 guitarists, banjoists, etc., must restring their instruments, which are designed wrong-way to…

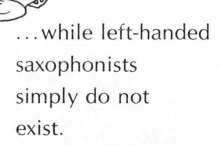

…while left-handed saxophonists simply do not exist.

Gum wrapper
openers are
right-handed...

...and so are
apple corers.

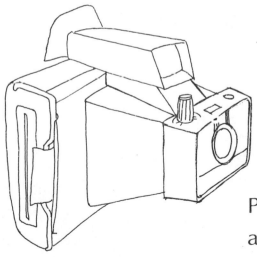

Polaroid cameras
are so right-handed
it's ridiculous.

Something as simple as a
frying pan

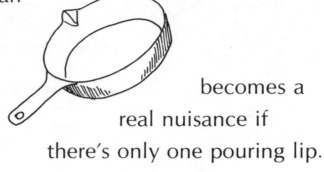

becomes a
real nuisance if
there's only one pouring lip.

It's always on the wrong side.

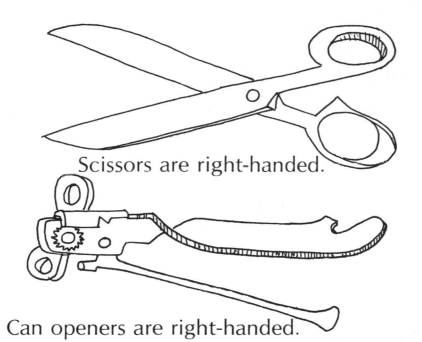

Scissors are right-handed.

Can openers are right-handed.

And so are wrist watches.

A more complicated tool can be a
downright menace. This typical power
saw, for
example. A
left-hander
must cross
his arms
to operate
it. Since
he can't see
where he's
going, he'll
either saw

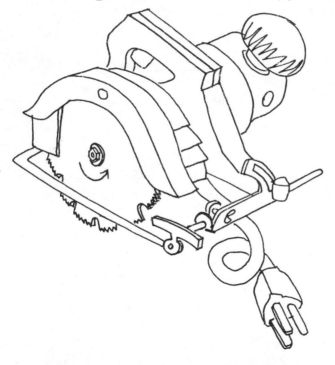

a crooked line, or chop off a couple
of fingers.

Consider the RIFLE: the
bolt action variety that
bolts the wrong way,

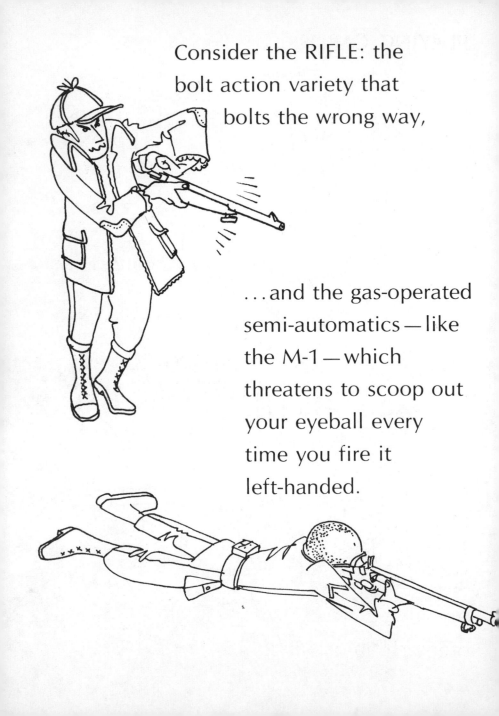

...and the gas-operated
semi-automatics — like
the M-1 — which
threatens to scoop out
your eyeball every
time you fire it
left-handed.

PLAYING CARDS:

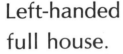

Left-handed
full house.

Same hand, considerably
improved by moving it
to the right.

(Are you beginning to get the picture?)

ADDING MACHINES...and SUBTRACTING
MACHINES:

(note position of handle.)

And then there's READING and WRITING:

Left-handers, who make up only 10% of the population, account for almost half the students in remedial reading courses. No one is sure why this is the case, but most experts agree it stems from the fact that in the western world words go left to right.

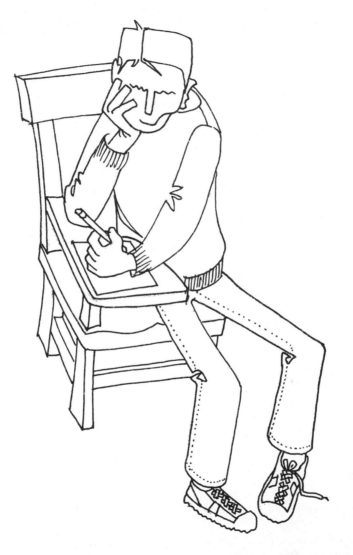

The less said about left-handed
writing, the better.

Why are things so
tough on left-handers?
Because a lot of people
who ought to know
better, believe left-
handers are an insignifi-
cant minority.

H. G. Wells, who CERTAINLY ought to have known better, believed left-handedness was insignificant, **and always had been.** He wrote: "WE KNOW [NEANDERTHAL MEN] WERE RIGHT-HANDED, LIKE MODERN MEN, BECAUSE THE LEFT SIDE OF THE BRAIN...WAS BIGGER THAN THE RIGHT." This is nonsense.

Virtually all of the evidence
shows that in prehistoric times...

THE NUMBER OF
LEFT-HANDERS
JUST ABOUT
EQUALED THE
NUMBER OF
RIGHT-HANDERS!

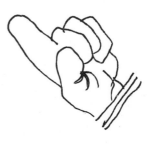

For instance, if Neanderthal men were exclusively right-handed, they would have invented right-handed tools, correct? Instead, they invented **ambidextrous** tools, suitable for either hand:

hammers,

saws,

axes,

pails,

pottery,

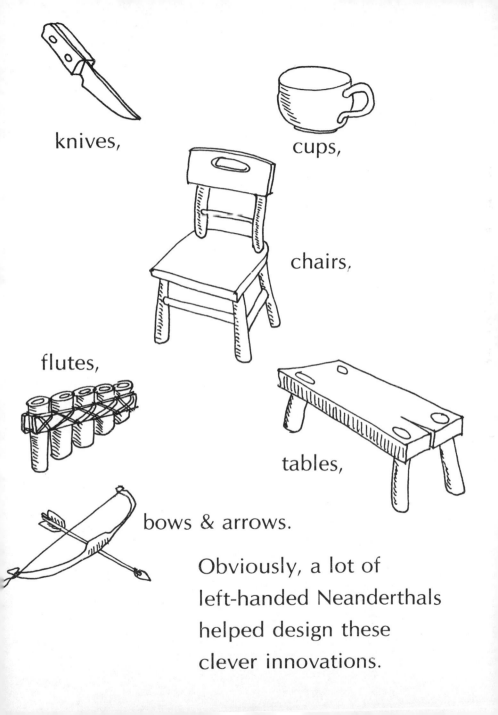

knives,

cups,

chairs,

flutes,

tables,

bows & arrows.

Obviously, a lot of
left-handed Neanderthals
helped design these
clever innovations.

Throughout much of ancient
history, the left-handers had
equal rights:

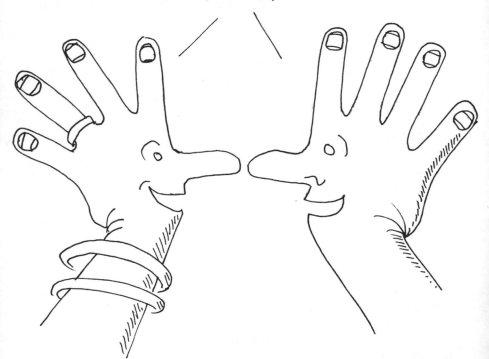

one good hand
deserves another!

This was even true in writing...

The Egyptians didn't feel
they had to write left
to right. They wrote up,
down, left **or** right,
depending on whim.

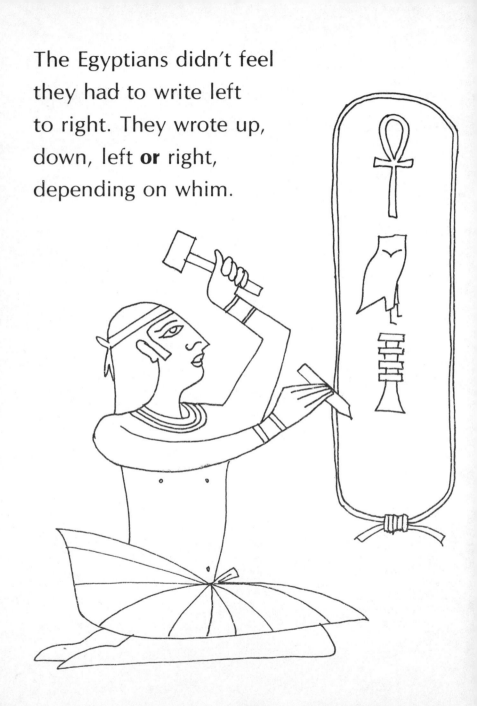

The Greeks wrote BOUSTROPHEDON style,
with each line alternating down the page,
like an ox plowing a field:
first line left to right,
next line right to left,
then another left to right

etcete

The Chinese, even to this day, write in vertical columns from right to left, which would indicate a slightly left-handed preference.

BIBLICAL NOTE: The Israelites were twice defeated by a Benjaminite army of "700 picked men who were left-handed." So much for you, Mr. H. G. Wells!

Actually, it was the Romans who
made up all the rules against
left-handers. They were the most
militantly right-handed people
in history.

Romans invented the
right-handed handshake...

...the fascist salute...

...and that left to right alphabet
that still causes a lot of trouble:

ABCDEFGHI
KLMNOPQ
RSTVWXYZ

The Roman word
for <u>right</u> was:

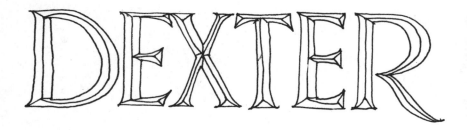

Their word for
<u>left</u> was:

SINISTER

Is it any wonder
left-handedness went
out of style?

In the Dark Ages, after the Roman Empire collapsed, a lot of people gave up reading, writing, shaking hands and saluting, and went back to being left-handed. Once again, the tools invented in this period reflect a general ambidextrality.

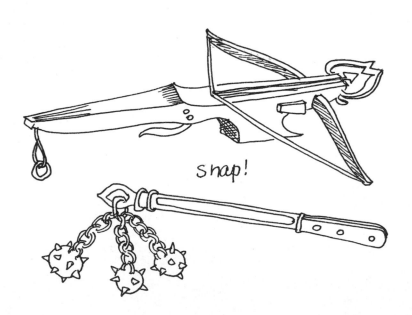

snap!

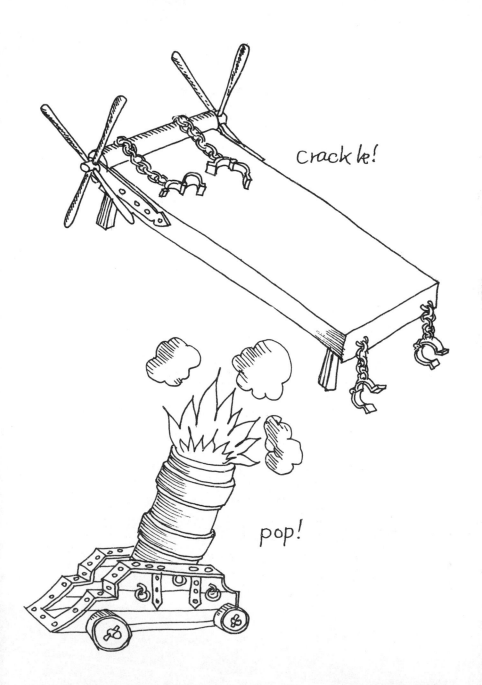

crackle!

pop!

MIDDLE EASTERN FOOTNOTE:
The Arabs have always insisted you eat with your right hand. This taboo isn't really directed against left-handers, but stems solely from certain social problems that arise where water is scarce. Some time back in history, they decided that the left hand should be reserved for certain hygienic purposes, the intensely personal nature of which made that hand particularly unsuitable for the communal dinner pot.

To show their impartiality, Arabs write left-handedly:

Today, we're right back where we were with the Romans. Just about everything's right-handed. Take jet planes. The pilot sits on this side so he can operate the all-important center control panel.

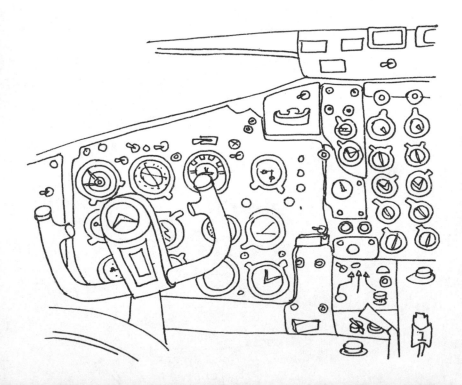

But what if the pilot's left-handed? He'd be more efficient on this side, but he's not allowed to sit here. Is this the safest possible arrangement?

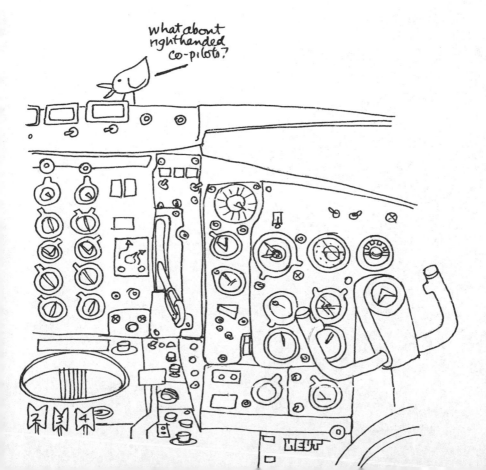

what about righthanded co-pilots?

THIS IS YOUR PILOT, LEFTY JONES...
WE ARE NOW CRUISING AT 30,000 FEET,
AT A SPEED OF...

If everything's so right-handed, wouldn't it make sense to train left-handers to be right-handed? Psychologists say "no"...it makes them stutter and things like that.

So, what's the answer? ———▷

A LEFTHANDED

Be it resolved that
all LEFT-THINKING
citizens, mindful that
their BIRTHLEFT
has been denied them,
shall henceforth
stand up for their
LEFTS! We call

MANIFESTO!

upon each one of them to support this BILL OF LEFTS, and specifically to...

BUY LEFT!

Purchase only left-handed products!

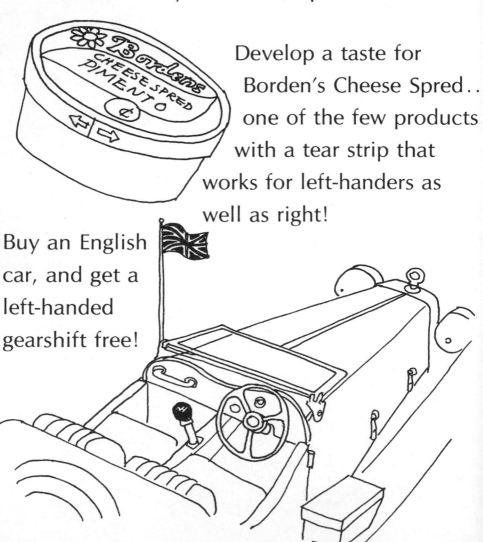

Develop a taste for
Borden's Cheese Spred..
one of the few products
with a tear strip that
works for left-handers as
well as right!

Buy an English
car, and get a
left-handed
gearshift free!

Insist on left-handed
check books!

And buy a typewriter —
the only left-handed
machine in general
use! (Most of
the important
keys are
on the
left.)

PATRONIZE LEFT

Purchase only the works of left-handers!

PLAY LEFT!

Return baseball to its pre-eminence as the great American pastime! (It favors left-handers.)

The lefthanded batter faces first base when he's completed his swing... and has a head start in running out his hit. 32% of all major league batters are lefthanded.

A lefthanded pitcher can
'keep an eye on first base
during his wind-up, and
cut down a runner's lead.
30% of all major league
pitchers are southpaws.

The lefthanded first baseman
can cover a tremendous area
of the infield with his right
(gloved) hand. Also, he's got an
advantage throwing to second
for the double play. 48% of all
major league first basemen are
lefthanded.

BUT...
there are
absolutely no
lefthanded
catchers!

Most important…

ACT LEFT!

Don't knuckle under! You've made
enough adjustments!

EAT LEFT! Let the other people
at the counter worry for a change!
RELAX LEFT! If you can't get a
left-handed tool for the job…
forget it!

WRITE LEFT! Write backwards!
No one can read it, but
with a little practice,
you'll find it a lot
easier for you!

REMEMBER! There are at least TWENTY
MILLION left-handed Americans! Singly,
they can do nothing, but UNITED...

...they can change the world!

COMES THE REVOLUTION...

...don't be left out.

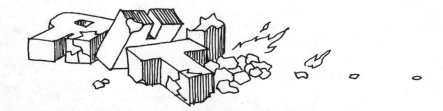